lasting impressions

Colin Campbell Cooper

This catalogue is published in conjunction with the exhibition
Lasting Impressions: Colin Campbell Cooper
June 24, 2010 to October 9, 2010
Organized by the Santa Barbara Historical Museum

© 2010 Santa Barbara Historical Museum
136 East De la Guerra Street, Santa Barbara, CA 93101
Telephone (805) 966-1601 • Fax (805) 966-1603
www.santabarbaramuseum.com

ISBN: 0-9704940-8-4

Exhibition Guest Curator: Marlene R. Miller
Catalogue Design: Garcin Media Group
Editors: Warren Miller and Michael Redmon
Printing and Binding: Jano Graphics, Ventura, CA
Photographs pp. 45, 49: Scott McClaine

Front cover:
A Santa Barbara Courtyard, c1925

Back cover:
Untitled – Blue Mandarin Coat

lasting impressions

Colin Campbell Cooper

SANTA BARBARA HISTORICAL MUSEUM

acknowledgements

THIS EXHIBITION IS MADE POSSIBLE THANKS TO THE GENEROUS SUPPORT OF

Sally & David Martin

Eleanor Van Cott

Astrid & Larry T. Hammett

Marlene & Warren Miller

Louise Clarke & John Carbon

Keith J. Mautino

William S. Burtness

Mr. & Mrs. Frederick C. Groos, Jr.

Paul & Kathleen Bagley

contents

Colin Campbell Cooper, shown here on board RMS *Carpathia* following the rescue of survivors from RMS *Titanic*, April 1912. Note Cooper's two paintings depicting the rescue efforts. Courtesy Sullivan Goss-An American Gallery, Santa Barbara.

foreword

William H. Gerdts, Ph.D.

Of all the major American Impressionist painters, Colin Campbell Cooper remains the only one to have divided his career equally between the East and West coasts of the United States. Some California artists, such as William Ritschel in Monterey, maintained studios in New York City, and others, from Chicago, such as William Wendt, remained loyal to their former hometown; some Eastern painters visited and painted fine, important pictures in the West, such as Childe Hassam in both California and Oregon. But Cooper was unique in not only seeking out the most vibrant aspects of his two primary areas of residency, but in establishing his reputation in identifying their unique but very contrasting visual qualities and appeal.

Cooper's greatest fame rests upon his architectural paintings of American cities: his native Philadelphia, Pittsburgh, Washington, D.C. and Chicago, but especially those of the skyline and individual skyscraper buildings of New York, constructed in the first decades of the twentieth century. While Hassam had been the most celebrated painter of that city in the last decade of the nineteenth century, and did paint some marvelous pictures in the following years, Cooper became his unparalleled successor in documenting what was referred to in books, magazines, and newspapers as "The new New York." In that, Cooper was a very "modern" artist, for though the Impressionist aesthetic was dominant rather than avant-garde during these years, his subject matter reflected the upward growth of the architecturally contemporary metropolis. In the larger sense, of course,

Cooper was more than this—he was the nation's leading painter of magnificent architecture—whether great cathedrals and churches in Europe, the magnificent buildings of India and Burma, or the enchanting buildings of the Panama-California Exposition held in San Diego in 1915-16. Awesome too are his pictures of California natural splendor of Yosemite which he visited on this trip, bringing a twentieth century aesthetic to the great tradition of commemorating that site, one which harkened back to Albert Bierstadt as well as a host of other artists from the 1860s on. As Marshall Price discusses in his essay in this catalogue, though, Cooper's New York pictures were not only about the transformation of the metropolis, but also about the interaction of its populace with this new urban environment.

The San Diego and Yosemite paintings were created during a visit to California. When he settled in Santa Barbara permanently in January, 1921, after the death of his wife, he transferred his commitment from buildings to gardens—those of the great new hostelries of California. The change may seem abrupt, though further study and surveys may reveal otherwise, for the least studied aspect of Cooper's career is the paintings he created in the later 1910s—when he appears to have moved away from the tall towers of Manhattan to time-honored New England structures such as those on Martha's Vineyard, mirroring a commitment to American tradition which had been espoused by Hassam and other of his fellow Impressionists. In California, Cooper's respect for tradition found a new outlet in his many renderings of the ruins of the San Juan Capistrano Mission, probably the edifice most often depicted by scores of California artists. Still, "newness" remained very much a part of the drawer to Cooper's California subject matter, the Samarkand and El Encanto hotels being themselves recently minted structures. Cooper's mission paintings, too, often focus as much on the colorful gardens as they do on the structure itself, contrasting the temporality of man's monuments with the ever-blooming glories of nature.

In addition to this involvement with brilliant colored, highly decorative hotel garden and mission pictures, Cooper's move to California released him from the overriding commitment which dominated his architectural paintings. He also continued to create figure paintings which he had successfully undertaken at the beginning of his career, and resumed with a new decorative emphasis in his later years in New York, and also created lovely floral still lifes.

As Deborah Solon discusses in her essay here, Santa Barbara offered Cooper not only an exceptionally pleasurable environment—though he seems to have paid relatively little interest to either its natural beauty or its historic mission—but also appreciative patronage and an opportunity for meaningful teaching at the Santa Barbara School of the Arts which had been founded just the year before he came. The School also offered Cooper the colleagueship of a group of exceptionally talented fellow painters—Fernand Lungren, DeWitt Parshall, Carl Oscar Borg, Belmore Browne, and John Marshall Gamble; in descriptions of the Santa Barbara art world, Cooper often shared the title of "Dean of Santa Barbara Artists" with Gamble.

Still, his old interest and ties were not forgotten. He returned to Europe in 1923 to renew his commitment to old monumental architecture, now adding Spain to his repertory, and he continued to explore and document the towers and skyline of New York on his return visits. Nor did he desert his principal exhibition outlet, continuing to display his work at the annual shows of the National Academy of Design, though not as frequently as he had during his New York years. Still, Cooper's primary venues were now in California—in San Diego, Los Angeles, Pasadena, and of course, Santa Barbara. On his death, in 1937, he was eulogized in newspapers across the country—remembered still as a major artist in both East and West.

William H. Gerdts, Ph.D. is Professor Emeritus of Art History, Graduate School of the City University of New York. Recipient of numerous academic and professional honors, Dr. Gerdts is the author of more than twenty-five books on American art, including *American Impressionism* (1984, 2nd edition, 2001) *Art Across America* (1990), and *California Impressionism* (1998). An honorary member of the Salmagundi Club, he was on the board of The American Art Journal, and remains on the boards of The American Art Review and the International Foundation for Art Research, and serves on the Board of Trustees of the Hudson River Museum, Yonkers, NY.

introduction

Marlene R. Miller, Guest Curator

One important aspect of the Santa Barbara Historical Museum's mission is to document and celebrate the cultural history of the community, which cannot be accomplished without paying tribute to those artists who have played such an important role in Santa Barbara's past.

For nearly two decades beginning in 1920, the nucleus of that artistic community was the Santa Barbara School of the Arts, and last year's exhibition, *Guiding Lights*, honored the School's most prominent faculty members. It is the Museum's goal to showcase each of these artist-teachers in a solo exhibition; *Lasting Impressions: Colin Campbell Cooper* is the first in this series. It is most gratifying to me to present this exhibition, and I am honored to serve once again as guest curator.

Cooper's name is synonymous with American Impressionism, and his paintings offer us a virtual world tour as seen through the eyes of a gifted traveler. By the time Cooper came to Santa Barbara in 1921, his national and international reputation—especially as a painter of monumental buildings—was well established. His last sixteen years spent here were filled with a variety of activities and interests. He was appointed Dean of Painting at the School of the Arts and was welcomed in Santa Barbara's social circles. In his own words, he found the atmosphere in Santa Barbara so conducive to the sort of atmosphere a painter most craves: agreeable climate, plenty of sunshine, flowers, mountains and seascapes, not to mention friends interested in all sorts of artistic endeavor.

Many people deserve a special acknowledgment for this exhibition. I would like to thank the individuals and institutions that have loaned their works, including the Dallas Museum of Art, The Irvine Museum, the New-York Historical Society, the Reading Public Museum, the Santa Barbara Museum of Art and the City of Santa Barbara. My heartfelt thanks also go to the sponsors whose support has made this exhibition and catalogue possible.

Catalogues such as this not only help viewers appreciate each exhibition; they also serve as an educational resource and historical record. Special recognition must go to Dr. William H. Gerdts, who wrote the insightful foreword; to Marshall N. Price, and Dr. Deborah Epstein Solon for their most informative essays; to Gloria Rexford Martin for her research of the previously unlocated painting of Pennsylvania Avenue; to Frank Goss and Jeremy Tessmer of Sullivan Goss-An American Gallery for their assistance and expertise; to Michael Redmon, the Historical Museum's Director of Research, and my husband, Warren, for their expert editing.

Lastly I also extend my gratitude to Daniel C. Calderon, Curator, and Juan Cervantes, Director of Facilities, for their professional installation, and—speaking as a Museum trustee—to Executive Director David Bisol for his leadership and vision.

Sydney Logan's House, pen and ink

The Boarding House, 1881, pen and ink

Courtesy private collection, Santa Barbara

impressions of new york

Marshall N. Price

The tragic events of September 11, 2001 that so horrified people throughout the nation also affected, dramatically and permanently, what is arguably the most recognized skyline in the world. In an instant, the zenith of a

Flat Iron Building

veritable mountain range of structures in lower Manhattan, the symbol of great economic and architectural achievement, was toppled. One effect has been, and will continue to be for some time, a general reassessment of the architecture of the skyscraper. Colin Campbell Cooper, Philadelphia-born and educated in the United States and Europe, received his earliest critical acclaim by capturing the beauty in such structures at a time when skyscrapers—new marvels of engineering—were recognized by few for their aesthetic qualities.

Colin Campbell Cooper was born in 1856 to Dr. Colin Campbell Cooper and Emily Williams Cooper. It was likely Cooper's mother, an amateur watercolorist, who first encouraged his interest in the arts. This inclination was bolstered when he attended the Centennial Exposition in Philadelphia in 1876. "The Art Gallery was of course a revelation, and yet of all the pictures which I distinctly remember a very horrible torture scene in the Inquisition was the one that made the greatest impression on me."[1] Cooper's father was also encouraging, and, when asked by his son about pursuing a career as a painter—different from that which his father intended, he replied, "Yes, my boy, if you have the feeling that you would make a success in another line of work than what you are doing now, go ahead."[2] Cooper, however, needed little encouragement to pursue his interest in art, and at age twenty-three he enrolled in the Pennsylvania Academy of the Fine Arts. He continued his training, as did many American artists of his generation, in Europe, at the Académies Julian, Delecluse, and Viti.[3]

Cooper returned to the States and received critical acclaim, first on the East Coast with his paintings of New York, Philadelphia, and other cities, and later on the West Coast, beginning with the Panama-Pacific International Exposition in 1915.[4] It was during the first decade or so after his return from Europe, between the years 1903 and 1914, that he recorded the changing face of a city and captured his impressions of New York.

By the 1890s, the production of skyscrapers in New York was roaring along. The steeple of Trinity Church, erected in 1846 and once the highest point in the city, was beginning to be dwarfed by edifices of industrialism and

This essay is based on one which appeared in the exhibition catalogue for Colin Campbell Cooper: Impressions of New York, curated by Mr. Price at the Santa Barbara Museum of Art, 2002.

commerce. In 1894, architectural historian and critic Barr Ferree wrote "... the typical modern city is becoming an assemblage of gigantic commercial buildings which overtop the loftiest church spire, and render insignificant the most ambitious and ornamental structures of an earlier time."[5] Indeed, Ferree must have been thinking of Trinity Church, which was eclipsed in height by the Manhattan Life Insurance building that same year. This was further followed by a succession of ever taller structures, each surpassing its predecessor. By 1902, no fewer than sixty-six skyscrapers had risen above lower Manhattan—most grouped within a few blocks of one another around Wall Street, where real estate prices now

Mountains of Manhattan

spiraled into the stratosphere, making land beneath the towers the most valuable property on earth.[6]

This assemblage of gigantic buildings is perhaps best seen in Cooper's *Mountains of Manhattan*. From a high vantage point, Cooper employs a sweeping view of lower Manhattan, using the unmistakable bulbous cupola of the Singer Building as the apex of the composition. The buildings, or "foothills," in the foreground are depicted in relative darkness and dissected by a small canyon (presumably West Street), while the "mountains," or middleground buildings, are bathed in the cool industrial haze of an early winter morning. Grouped as they

are, it is difficult to identify individual structures (with a few notable exceptions, such as the Singer building); they create a continuous mountain range of structures running through lower Manhattan.

While Cooper was not the first artist to paint the urban landscape, he was one of the earliest to recognize the aesthetic qualities inherent in skyscrapers.[7] As Dr. William Gerdts writes in his illuminating essay in *East Coast / West Coast and Beyond: Colin Campbell Cooper, American Impressionist*,

> Daniel Burnham's Flat Iron Building of 1902 was the most painted, printed, photographed, and illustrated of all American buildings. Though not ever the tallest building in the city, it aroused great curiosity and celebrity, and on completion was referred to as "the slenderest" and "the most aquiline" of structures, likened to a ship's prow, and, like the canyons of lower Manhattan, thus absorbed into a traditional pictorial metaphor. The structure drew admiration not only for its distinct triangular shape, necessarily conforming to the ground plan of the avenue crossing, but also its location at the intersection of the city's most renowned avenues: Fifth Avenue and Broadway.[8]

The skyscraper aesthetic (or lack thereof) was at the center of a debate between architectural critics. Often using as their medium popular journals of the day such as *Scribner's Magazine*, *The Booklover's Magazine*, *The Century Magazine*, and others, critics could reach a fairly broad cross-section of the general public. Even a brief foray into the early historiography of the skyscraper criticism at the time of Cooper's paintings illuminates an early debate over the skyscraper aesthetic and eventually a shift in taste *toward* the aesthetic of these buildings.

Montgomery Schuyler, perhaps the most outspoken architectural critic of the early twentieth century, began a crusade against the skyscraper in his 1903 article, "The Skyscraper Problem." And, while Schuyler recognized the inevitability of building tall, it was both the (seeming) lack of historical foundation upon which skyscrapers were built and extreme height to which he most objected. "The extreme skyscraper that we know and disrespect presents in its front an obviously irrelevant compilation of historical architecture, while its equally conspicuous sides and rear make no pretensions to architecture at all."[9]

By 1908, Schuyler's "To Curb the Skyscraper," the second in a series of three articles between 1903-1913, conceded the permanence of this type of building but called for strict guidelines on the treatment of the architectural detail.

Schuyler's initial dislike, later acceptance (reluctant though it was), and eventual defense of the skyscraper reflect a larger acceptance and appreciation of the buildings themselves. By 1913, in "The Towers of Manhattan and Notes on the Woolworth Building" (the third article in the series), Schuyler has reevaluated his earlier assessment and, while not showering these buildings with praise, he gives them modest laudatory comments: "It will be admitted that all these towers are shapely, worthy of attention which they compel, credits to their designers, ornaments to the city...."[10]

When completed in 1913, the Woolworth Building became the most dominant feature of the New York skyline; at fifty-seven stories, it was the tallest building in the world. Cooper used it as the subject of a number of works, often choosing to depict the towering skyscraper at a distance, as seen in *Hudson River Waterfront*, where he frames the colorful scene with the Woolworth Building on the left and the darker but equally imposing

Hudson River Waterfront

Singer Building on the right. Schuyler eventually had to concede that it was the design of the tower, and "... the lightening of detail, which has converted it into the thing of beauty which we now thankfully recognize."[11] It is impossible to know whether Cooper was aware of Schuyler's writings on architecture, but he was one of the first to recognize the beauty inherent in these structures, long before Schuyler.

Cooper was an assiduous student of composition. He combined this with an emphasis on the importance of direct notation of subject. This may have been due to his academic training at the Pennsylvania Academy under Thomas Eakins (himself a diligent student of composition). In 1909, Cooper wrote for *Palette and Bench*, "I cannot say that I would advise the use of canvas instead of paper or the painting of opaque rather than transparent watercolors; though the former has several advantages, particularly in that the effect may be more directly noted than with the transparent colors on paper—much as one is able to do with oil colors—and therefore it is especially useful for making studies and sketches."[12] Reference to Cooper's essay, "Skyscrapers and How to Build them in Paint," is essential in understanding how he composed his paintings. It is an invaluable resource, as it details not only materials and composition but also color relationships and perspective—it is, in effect, a technical manifesto on the painting of skyscrapers.

Cooper realized that the verticality of tall buildings often offers an inherent frame for a composition, and he utilized a simple device to aid him.

> The younger student is apt to feel discouraged before a great pile of buildings and irregular angles. He has perhaps been instructed in the ordinary rules of perspective ... this knowledge will be useful, no doubt, but not essential in making a sketch perspective. The well known device of cutting an oblong hole in a piece of cardboard and holding it at a greater or less distance from the eye will bound the composition of the picture it is proposed to make.[13]

A number of his works show the employment of this method, including *Fifth Avenue, New York City* and *The Financial District*. In each, the artist, using a not-so-sophisticated device to map out the territory, developed a sophisticated diagram of horizontal and vertical lines based on the outline of the buildings in the view (often around the most prominent middle-distance building). This basic diagram was then used in turn to establish the relationship of the various geometric shapes (essentially the buildings) created by the lines, thereby establishing the general composition. It was not a method that Cooper invented; in fact, it had been employed for centuries. "This method eliminates the necessity of employing a horizon line with vanishing points except so far as we must have a point toward which we face in making our measurements or taking the horizontals; we will call this, for want of better term, the 'facing point'...."[14] It

was an efficient method—instead of first establishing a vanishing point, Cooper established the parameters of the composition, and the vanishing point would then reveal itself.

The second part of Cooper's thesis delves into the importance and uses of color. "The very first consideration in this question of color of a picture is not the local colors of things but *the color of the light which illumens* [sic] *these things.*"[15] Cooper was just as methodical with color as he

The Financial District

was with regard to composition. In *The Financial District* and *Fifth Avenue, New York City*, we may observe his method at work. He writes, "Should the effect chosen be of grey weather the problem [of coloring] becomes somewhat simpler, the contrasts being not so forcible. In general the illuminating light from the sky on a grey day is cool grey color; now the opposite or complementary of cool grey would be warm grey. So the shadow will be warm in proportion as the light is cold."[16]

> ...whether it be Maiden Lane or Madison Square, the architectural canyons of lower New York or the Cathedral gates of England that he [Cooper] paints, his every canvas has a charm and an interest that inhere in the scene and awe wholly apart from the beauty that it attaches to a particular effect of atmosphere or season. Hence his

specialty can never breed the monotony which suggests that many canvases are segments of a larger whole—each has its own wonderful details, its own grand suggestions, its own poetic message.[17]

While paintings of skyscrapers first brought Cooper critical success, he was equally adept at capturing images of city life. Architecture had long been a subject of interest to him, and he used it as a backdrop, upon which he depicted the character of the city by composing a range of pictures expressing the diversity inherent in New York.

Cooper's New York is one of vast cityscapes and lone skyscrapers; of the urban bustle of downtown denizens and barren corners of mid-town tranquility; of buildings as poetic embodiments of industrialism and a backdrop for the diversity of the city. Each painting, regardless of subject, is a part, or stanza, of an epic poem, perhaps best described in Cooper's own words:

> The meaning behind my pictures would be precisely the same if I painted wooded hills and mountain torrents. They cannot say but the same thing, for they are all part of the poem of life. The only difference is in the metre. Here in New York it is tuned to a quicker, more strident music, but the song it sings does not vary. I hope that I catch that stridency in my pictures, but much more I hope that I catch the notes of the song behind it, for that is the important thing.[18]

From the movements of his oil sketches to the concertos of fully realized canvases, these are the elements that compose a symphony—and Colin Campbell Cooper's impressions of New York.

Marshall Price is the Curator of Modern and Contemporary Art at the National Academy Museum in New York City; until 2002, he was Assistant Curator at the Santa Barbara Museum of Art and has held positions at the Chesapeake Bay Maritime Museum and the Walters Art Museum. He has organized numerous exhibitions and written and lectured widely on American art of the nineteenth, twentieth and twenty-first centuries. A specialist in 1930s abstraction in America, he is currently completing his Ph.D. at The Graduate Center, City University of New York.

NOTES:

1. Autobiographical Notes. Santa Barbara Museum of Art artist file, Santa Barbara Museum of Art, 1. Also, for a fairly complete biographical essay, a chronology of awards and exhibitions, and professional affiliations, see James M. Hansen, Colin Campbell Cooper, exhibition catalogue, Santa Barbara, 1981.

2. Colin Campbell Cooper, "The Picture that First Helped Me to Success," *New York Times*, 28 January 1912, sec. 3, 5.

3. Cooper spent nearly fourteen years in Europe during this time. He returned to the U.S. around 1901; however, he continued to travel the world, including Europe and Asia, throughout his life. He would eventually make Santa Barbara his permanent residence in 1921. See Hansen, *Colin Campbell Cooper.*

4. In 1915 Cooper won both a gold medal and a silver medal at the Panama-Pacific International Exposition.

5. Barr Ferree, "The High Building and Its Art," *Scribner's Magazine* 15, no. 3 (March 1894): 297.

6. Ric Burns and James Sanders, *New York: An Illustrated History* (New York: Knopf, 1999), 238.

7. Cooper was the first to paint certain buildings. See Bruce Weber, *The Prowed Tower*, exhibition catalogue, Berry-Hill Galleries, 2.

8. William H. Gerdts and Deborah Epstein Solon, *East Coast/West Coast and Beyond, Colin Campbell Cooper, American Impressionist*, Laguna Art Museum, Laguna Beach, CA, 2006: 46

9. Schuyler, "The Skyscraper Problem," *Scribner's Magazine* 34, no. 2 (August, 1903), 254.

10. Montgomery Schuyler, "The Towers of Manhattan and Notes on the Woolworth Building," *Architectural Record* 33 (February 1913): 104.

11. Ibid., 108.

12. Colin Campbell Cooper, "Skyscrapers and How to Build them in Paint," *Palette and Bench* 1 no. 5 (January 1909): 90.

13. Ibid., 91–92.

14. Ibid., 92.

15. Colin Campbell Cooper, "Skyscrapers and How to Build them in Paint", *Palette and Bench* 1, no. 6 (February 1909): 106. Cooper's italics.

16. Ibid., 107.

17. Willis E. Howe, "The Work of Colin Campbell Cooper," *Brush and Pencil* 18, no. 2 (August 1906): 73–75.

18. Louis Baury, "The Message of Manhattan," *Bookman* (August 1911): 594.

The artist's bungalow, 1715 Anacapa Street, Santa Barbara

california and beyond

Deborah Epstein Solon, Ph.D.

By the second decade of the twentieth century, Colin Campbell Cooper's career and reputation were well established. Residing in New York, his fame rested on his splendid skyscraper paintings and his celebratory images of the modern city—but a series of events that unfolded during the teens would radically change his life by 1920.

Cooper and his wife, Emma, traveled extensively, chiefly throughout Europe, in the early years of their marriage and into the twentieth century. However, their most exotic trip was undoubtedly to India. According to Cooper's diary, the couple left New York on October 11, 1913. Traveling via Italy and through the Suez Canal, they arrived in India by early November and remained abroad until mid-March of the following year, retracing their route through the Suez Canal and returning via France to America.

India was hardly a common tourist destination for American artists—even the most seasoned and intrepid —despite the fact that the actual journey had been made somewhat easier by the opening of the Suez Canal in 1869.

Cooper's diary is a travelogue of their journey, which included the cities Bombay, Ahmedabad, Udaipur, Jaipur, Delhi, Agra, Benares, Darjeeling, Calcutta, Rangoon, and Madras. "Certainly, for the most part," he

This essay is based on one which appeared in *East Coast / West Coast and Beyond, Colin Campbell Cooper, American Impressionist*, published on the occasion of the exhibition of the same name organized by Laguna Art Museum, Laguna Beach, CA, 2006.

wrote in his final diary entry for the trip, "we have enjoyed our experiences. I do not say that I do not care to go back again."[1] The Coopers remained in France

Palace Gate, Udaipur, India

through the summer of 1914 and the outbreak of World War I, where he worked up the studies made in situ. He outlined his progress in a letter to the New York dealer William Macbeth:

> We are here in this little fishing village near Marseilles, engaged in elaborating the studies onto canvas and I have made a good start toward getting together at least ten pictures of good importance of India. I am hoping that I may be able to show these together as a collection more or less.... It may be of course that you will not care for my work, but supposing that you were pleased with it, what prospect would there be for an exhibition

at your galleries say sometime in the early part of January?[2]

As the situation in Europe became increasingly volatile —Cooper was briefly arrested as a "German spy" for photographing the mobilization—the couple returned to New York in November.[3] Cooper again wrote to Macbeth:

Although Mrs. Cooper and I have been back in our studio for several weeks we have not really unpacked yet, being so busy with other things and there I have not had my India pictures in a condition to show you. I would be very glad, however, now to have you see what there is even though it may not be advisable to have an exhibition this season. One of the more important canvases, and perhaps the most complete is wanted by the Corcoran exhibition and I would like to have you see it before it goes....[4]

Impressed, Macbeth organized a show of Cooper's India pictures that opened in February 1915. Included were two versions of the Taj Mahal, *The Taj Mahal, Agra (Afternoon)*, and *The Taj Mahal, Agra (Morning)*. While Cooper was critical of Indian architecture, noting a "sameness about their mosques, minarets, and pavilions that is somewhat disappointing," he was overwhelmed by the Taj. "That has rare distinction," he noted.[5]

The Taj Mahal is arguably one of the most famous mausoleums in the world and the preeminent monument of the Mughal Empire (1526–1857).[6] Begun in 1630 and largely completed by 1653, its unique architectural construction includes a dome surrounded by four clustered kiosks and encased by four minarets.[7] Fashioned of white marble, jewel-encrusted, and adorned with intricate floral and geometric inlays in profuse surface detailing,

it is approached through gardens and monumental reflecting pools.

Taj Mahal, Afternoon

The gardens surrounding the Taj were an essential aspect of the site's architectural program. Known as the Chahar Bagh—Persian for Gardens of Paradise—the rectangular gardens are divided into four quadrants, four being a sacred number in Islam. Within these gardens are two main water channels that bisect at right angles. At the intersection of the channels is the main water tank, the Pool of Abundance, situated on a raised platform.

Typical views of the Taj generally include the main water channel. Cooper's view in *Taj Mahal, Afternoon* is slightly more elusive. The regal white palace emerges like an apparition from the landscape. However, the foreshortened reflecting pool in the foreground is not one of the main axial water channels. It may be that we are looking at a view from the west side of the water tank and one of the smaller reflecting pools.[8] Cooper established the viewer's perspective from literally "inside" the water, while the three figures help to indicate the scale of the 250-foot-high edifice. Cooper's flickering, Impressionist brushwork creates an overall light that saturates the building and casts shadows in the foreground. The effect is a shimmering pictorial approximation of how the interplay of light and shadow must have struck the visitor's eye.

Critics singled out the Taj Mahal paintings. "The chefs-de-oeuvre [sic] of the exhibition are of that highest expression of Indian architectural beauty, the Taj Mahal. Artists without number have exhausted their talents on its symmetry of design, the delicate grace of its domes, and the Arabian Nights atmosphere that surrounds it. Mr. Cooper has admirably depicted the inspiring structure and has embodied in his two pictures the romance of the East."[9]

When Cooper wrote to Macbeth in 1914 about the possibility of an exhibition, he especially wanted him to see "one of the more important canvases, and perhaps the most complete," which was wanted for exhibition by the Corcoran.[10] *Palace Gate, Udaipur, India* was indeed exhibited at the Corcoran Gallery of Art, but returned for the Macbeth exhibition.[11] The Coopers spent several weeks in Udaipur, where they witnessed a "procession" that may have inspired this painting.[12]

Udaipur is located in the southern part of what is now Rajasthan, the largest state in northwestern India. Perhaps the most renowned structure was the Lake Palace complex, which was accessed on one side through a massive, three-arched gate. Placed outside the great trefoil gate, the painting's viewer joins the procession slowly moving toward the palace grounds. Elephants with their howdahs, camels, horses, a swirl of humanity in vibrant costumes, are all beautifully described. Carefully articulated architectural structures are juxtaposed against mere dabs of color suggesting the staffage figures massed at the gates. One reviewer described it as "perhaps the most striking work in the display ... a re-

markable portrayal of the rich colored, strange life of an ancient city under tropic skies."[13] The painting's extensive exhibition history undoubtedly establishes it as one of Cooper's most acclaimed Indian works.[14]

In 1915, both Colin and Emma Cooper mounted a joint exhibition of their respective Indian pictures at the Memorial Art Gallery in Rochester.[15] Cooper's ten paintings included *Taj Mahal, Agra,* and *Palace Gate, Udaipur, India.*

Panama-Pacific Exposition

The Panama-Pacific International Exposition in San Francisco was one of the seminal events of 1915. Intended as a celebration of the completion of the Panama Canal, and marking the 400th anniversary of the discovery of the Pacific Ocean, it showcased San Francisco's phoenix-like resurgence from the rubble of the 1906 earthquake and fire. Opening on February 20 and running through December 4, 1915, the fair was a monumental enterprise.[16] Every state had a representative building on the 635-acre site; twenty-four nations participated, despite the fact that World War I was raging in Europe.[17]

The art pavilion, the Palace of Fine Arts, contained 113 galleries, housing thousands of paintings from all over the world. Among the American delegation were Childe Hassam, Frank Duveneck, William Merritt Chase, John Singer Sargent, and James McNeill Whistler. Cooper exhibited six works, receiving a gold medal for oil painting and a silver medal for watercolor.

The Coopers went to San Francisco to visit the exposition, probably in late 1915; he found many of the buildings apt subject matter. The one building that Cooper revisited in various iterations was the Palace of Fine Arts. Louis Christian Mulgardt, architect of the Court of the Ages and author of a critique of the architecture and landscape gardens characterized the building:

> The Palace of the Fine Arts is, in reality, not one complete building but four separate and distinct elements. The rotunda, an octagonal structure, forms the center of the composition. On either side is a detached peristyle which follows the curve of the gallery itself. As it describes an arch about the western shore of the Laguna…. The architecture, as a whole, is early Roman, with traces of the finer Greek influence.[18]

The Palace was the brainchild of San Francisco architect Bernard R. Maybeck, who sought to integrate it seamlessly within a timeless landscape. Set in the lagoon, the building was physically isolated from the rest of the exhibits. An eight-color pastel theme was enforced for all the architecture; the fine-arts building sported ocher and green columns, and burnt-orange Corinthian capitals and dome. The San Francisco exposition was commonly referred to as the Domed City (undoubtedly a subtle play on the Chicago's 1893 World's Columbian Exposition known as the White City), as several of the buildings

were domed. The profusely decorated Palace of Fine Arts was constructed to be viewed under different lighting conditions; Cooper, in fact, painted it under both natural and artificial illumination.

Cooper often made multiple versions of his images and gave them similar titles. One painting of the Palace of Fine Arts, *Panama-Pacific Exhibition*, includes a panoramic view from the shore. Cooper's virtuoso handling of full

Half Dome, Yosemite

sunlight and shadow on water and the impact of the pastel color scheme are especially resonant.

By March 1916, the artist had exhibited three paintings of Panama-Pacific Exposition subjects at the Oakland Public Museum and the Schussler Galleries in San Francisco.[19] Also that spring, he showed *Half Dome, Yosemite* at the Los Angeles Museum of History, Science and Art (now Los Angeles County Museum of Art). Cooper visited Yosemite National Park during his stay in Northern California. Nearly nine thousand feet high, Half Dome, located at the eastern end of Yosemite Valley, is part of the Sierra Nevada mountain range. From the vantage point of a stream at the base of the mountain,

Cooper painted a cool winter scene in lavenders, blues, and whites, but with warm shadows throughout. The mountain, a geological skyscraper, leaves its distinctive imprint on the horizon, nature's equivalent to the urban towers that Cooper so enthusiastically embraced. Nonetheless, Cooper's interest in grandiloquent landscapes was limited and later, when he relocated to California, his interest was in nature cultivated and civilized.

The Coopers spent several weeks in April 1916 in Los Angeles before continuing to San Diego.[20] En route, they stopped at the Mission San Juan Capistrano, one of a chain of twenty-one missions located throughout the state. Mission San Juan Capistrano was founded by Father Junípero Serra on November 1, 1776. Its great cathedral, completed in 1806, was reduced to rubble during Southern California's devastating earthquake on December 8, 1912.[21] By mid-century, the building had fallen into complete disrepair, its materials cannibalized for other structures. The mission was returned to the Church after California attained statehood, and by the 1860s the land around it was parceled out to homesteaders. When the Santa Fe Railway established a stop at Capistrano, the town was, quite literally, put "on the map."

With the railroad came real-estate developers, buyers, and tourists. The drive to salvage the mission was spearheaded by Charles Fletcher Lummis, whose California boosterism and propaganda flooded the pages of his magazine *The Land of Sunshine*.[22] Lummis's attempt to polish the mission's tarnished image, making it appealing to tourists, was couched in romantic tales and legends of its halcyon days.[23] Artists, by the early twentieth century, were already attracted to the aura of the ruins. According to scholar Jean Stern, interest crested by the mid-1920s, no doubt fueled by its geographic proximity to the art colony in Laguna Beach.[24] Among the many Impressionist

artists who painted at the mission were Anna Hills, Joseph Kleitsch, Guy Rose, Donna Schuster, Elmer Wachtel, and William Wendt.

Cooper, too, was seduced by Southern California's most historic buildings. His many paintings of the mission include *Mission San Juan Capistrano*, and *Mission Courtyard (San Juan Capistrano)*.[25] *Mission San Juan Capistrano*, a watercolor, is a foreshortened version of the same corridor. Cooper's facility with the medium is evident in the sunshine that penetrates the arches, creating shadows and highlights. And as if to remind viewers that this was a functioning parish, Cooper included a padre and altar boy. The painting was reproduced on the cover of *California Southland* for September 1927. The oil painting, *Mission Courtyard*, combines architectural elements with brightly colored vegetation.[26] Light bathes the canvas, capturing the mellow hues of the aging walls; dabs of strategically placed color suggest the blooms.

Interestingly, one mission to which Cooper appears not to have given much attention is the one in what was to become his new home city. The small watercolor, *Santa*

Mission San Juan Capistrano

An Afternoon Stroll, Balboa Park

Barbara Mission, is the one of the few extant paintings that Cooper did of this building.

By early May, the *Los Angeles Times* noted that Cooper had already spent a considerable amount of time in San Diego painting the "fair grounds," a reference to the Panama-California Exposition that opened in San Diego on January 1, 1915.[27]

The circumstances culminating in the San Diego fair were a bit complicated. In 1909, San Diego, San Francisco, and New Orleans were all lobbying the United States Congress to "host" an exposition to celebrate the opening of the Panama Canal. When the San Diego organizers realized that their bid for an international fair was futile, they agreed to support San Francisco over New Orleans in exchange for being allowed to sponsor a smaller fair demonstrating how industrial, agricultural, and commercial achievement could give rise to cities in the West. Ironically, the year-long Panama-California International Exposition opened as "international" on January 1, 1916.

The ambitious landscape program was originally given to John C. Olmsted and his brother Frederick Law Olmsted, Jr. (scions of the great designer Frederick Law Olmsted). The brothers were esteemed landscape designers in their own right, having laid the grounds for the 1905 Lewis and Clark Exposition and the 1909 Alaska-Yukon-Pacific Exposition. New York architect Bertram Goodhue was named supervisory architect, assisted by a local architect, Irving Gill.

Cooper painted several splendid watercolors of the exposition grounds. *An Afternoon Stroll (Pool and Canadian Building)* includes the pond in deep recession with the Canadian Building to the left. Originally known as the Commerce and Industries Building, it became the Canadian Building when the exposition went international. Cooper's facility as a watercolorist is made apparent in this beautiful rendition of buildings, the pond, and visitors to the fair on a glorious, sunny afternoon. It is likely that this picture was exhibited in 1916 at the Philadelphia Art Watercolor Exhibition, and at the American Watercolor Society in 1917.

The Coopers returned to New York in October 1916. The productive period in California had resulted in paintings of the architecture at both the San Francisco and San Diego fairs, part of the continuum originating with his European cathedrals, such as his depictions of the Beauvais and Malines Cathedrals, and extending through his skyscraper and India pictures. The paintings of approximately 1917-19 suggest a transition. While Cooper continued to exhibit skyscraper paintings throughout his career, his focus began to change, shifting from urban to more rural and nostalgic architecture and to figure paintings.

From New York to Washington, D.C., Philadelphia, and Rochester, Cooper had spent the first decade of the century spearheading scenes of urban architecture. That his oeuvre was so synonymous with this genre may have been a mixed blessing. In his own words, "to confine oneself to one class of subject seems to me to narrow the vision and limit the endeavor."[28] His renewed interest in figure paintings recalls his early academic roots, and his sensitivity as a portraitist.

The later figurative works reflect a different sensibility. His genteel women, occasionally wearing oriental costumes and holding parasols, set in gardens, boats, or fashionable parlors, undoubtedly relate to similar scenes popularized by artists of the "Giverny Group," such as Frederick Carl Frieseke, Richard Miller, and Lawton Parker.[29] While these artists also portrayed nudes, a subject Cooper eschewed, they painted images of women at leisure and dressed in beautiful costumes, articulated through Impressionist light and color. Although the group's popularity crested in the earlier teens, their influence endured.

Cooper's *The Mandarin Coat*, is a smaller version of the painting of the same name exhibited at the 1917 winter exhibition at the National Academy of Design and used as the cover illustration for *Town and Country Magazine* in March 1918. A tour-de-force, the intricately patterned floral designs of the figure's kimono and parasol are subtly echoed in the background floral garden setting. *The Rustic Gate*, exhibited at the 1918 winter exhibition of the National Academy of Design and at the Memorial Art Gallery in Rochester in 1919, also features a woman in a garden but this time enveloped by flowers. She stands within a trellis holding a red bouquet and gazes rather wistfully into the distance. For most of the paintings of this period, Cooper used paid models.

While Cooper's artistic focus was in the process of changing, his personal life took a dramatic turn with the death of his wife in 1920. Although no extant correspondence or diaries discuss her death from tuberculosis, her passing must have been a tremendous blow.[30] The two were constant companions for over twenty years.[31] Emma's death may have initiated Cooper's desire to begin a new life or at least change his surroundings. In the absence of any documentation, however, we can only speculate on why he moved to Santa Barbara, seemingly rather suddenly, in January 1921.

The Rustic Gate

Cooper's surprising decision must have looked like artistic suicide to his established East Coast colleagues. Cooper himself stated that in California he was "isolated from the artistic universe of America," and that "after spending nearly twenty years identified with the art life of New York, I miss the many friends with whom I was associated there."[32] By no means, however, did Cooper abandon New York, but maintained a studio there for ten years after he relocated.[33]

The notion that California was remote—an "island on the land," where artists toiled in relative isolation—was a refrain often repeated by both Eastern and Western critics.[34] Recent scholarship on Impressionists in California within the context of American Impressionism has proven that notion fatuous.[35] And Cooper's remarks can be seen as part of a persistent, exaggerated parlance that lingered throughout the twentieth century. At last, American art history is now beginning to debunk the concept of "synecdochic nationalism," whereby painting and painters on the East Coast were seen as representative of the entire country.[36] Like Cooper, many artists who worked in California maintained studios elsewhere, exhibited throughout the United States, and were associated with dealers in major cities. And they traveled frequently, both within the country and abroad, scarcely suffering any "tyranny of distance" from New York.[37] Cooper's exhibition history during his California years bears out his rather full participation in the artistic communities locally and farther afield.

Basket of Dahlias

It is certainly possible that Cooper visited Santa Barbara in 1916 when he traveled from San Francisco to San Diego. He later wrote that he found "Santa Barbara conducive to the sort of thing a painter craves—climate, flowers, mountains, seascapes, etc. with a community interested in all sorts of artistic matters."[38] In addition to exquisite scenery, it had an art colony that had been established in the late nineteenth century by the artist Alexander Harmer.[39] As in so many California cities, Santa Barbara's growth was the result of the railroads: a rail link completed in 1901 made the city easily accessible. Capitalizing on that accessibility, Harmer built a studio complex intended to entice artists in the hope of creating a colony. Over

the next two decades, the thriving colony included Thomas Moran, Fernand Lungren, Carl Oscar Borg, John Marshall Gamble, and Albert and Adele Herter.

Santa Barbara had two unique ingredients: a surrounding community of great wealth and an art school. Between 1890 and 1930, forty "great estates" were built in Santa Barbara and its neighboring community Montecito. These estates were home to families such as those of CKG Billings, George Owen Knapp, and Frederic Gould.[40] They funded civic projects, established exclusive day schools, and certainly could afford to patronize the arts. Perhaps more compelling for Cooper, the Santa Barbara School of the Arts, founded in 1920, adopted a mission to "develop a spirit of fellowship in the arts ... to lead the individual student to worthy achievement."[41] The art faculty included Fernand Lungren, De Witt Parshall, Carl Oscar Borg, Belmore Browne, and John Marshall Gamble. Although Cooper had not taught since his early years in Philadelphia, this may have been an opportunity to supplement his income, since the financial source of his fairly comfortable lifestyle remains unclear. By joining the faculty in 1921 to teach an outdoor landscape class, he was able to work in a convivial and beautiful environment, and his association bolstered the reputation of the nascent institution.

Believing that the gardens in Europe were "charming ... [but] I do not think that anywhere in the world will be found anything more exquisite in that respect than the gardens of California in Pasadena and Montecito," Cooper explored the Santa Barbara area.[42] By the early 1920s, there were several major resort hotels set on exquisitely landscaped grounds. El Encanto (The Enchanted), originally a group of small cottages, was transformed into a small hotel complex with the addition of a large central building. With views from the Channel Islands to the Goleta Valley, the grounds included native plants and large eucalyptus trees; the centerpiece was an Italian red brick pergola in a setting of small waterfalls and a lily pond.[43]

El Encanto's gardens became a favorite location for Cooper. He made several paintings of the pond and pergola. *The Lotus Pool, El Encanto, Santa Barbara* is a foreshortened, axial view from inside the pond looking out toward the pergola and the eucalyptus trees silhouetted in the distance. Cooper's established mastery of plein-air painting reaches a new level in works such as this. The lush landscape, drenched in sunlight and filled with an array of brightly colored flowers, underscores the tranquil ambience of the gardens. It is likely that this picture was exhibited at the Pennsylvania Academy of the Fine Arts in 1922.

The Samarkand Hotel (Persian for "land of heart's desire") was originally the site of a private boys school built by Dr. Prynce Hopkins in 1915. Surrounding the two-story main building with wings for dormitories and classrooms, its exotically planted garden terraces led to a large artificial lake. When the school failed in 1918, Hopkins's mother renovated the complex into a small, exclusive hotel catering to an Eastern clientele who summered in Santa Barbara. Its magnificent gardens attracted many, including Cooper. In *The Terrace at Samarkand*, profusions of plants in the ground and in pots overrun a terrace, creating a riot of color that contrasts with the blue, cloudless California sky.

In addition to painting hotel gardens, Cooper also depicted more intimate spaces, such as shown in *The Green Bench*, on the grounds of the Harmer Adobe where his studio was located, and *Santa Barbara Courtyard*. Depictions of

The Terrace at Samarkand

domestic gardens were common among East Coast Impressionists such as Edmund Greacen, George Burr, Clark Voorhees, and Childe Hassam.[44] The "Grandmother's Garden," a symbol of home and hearth, had become a pictorial metaphor for conservative values and family life in the early twentieth century.[45] And while Cooper's scenes are not their exact pictorial equivalent, they are certainly closer in spirit than the uncultivated landscapes favored by so many Impressionist artists in California.

In March 1922, Cooper returned to New York to serve on the award's jury for the 97th Annual Exhibition of the National Academy of Design, but by September, he was once again in San Diego visiting friends.[46] The following May, Cooper made a nearly ten-month-long trip to Spain.[47] His sporadic trip diary records stops in Segovia, Seville, Madrid, Granada, Pedrago, and Burgos. In Madrid, he "paid his respects to the Prado," and he found Segovia a "wonderfully picturesque town."[48] He returned to America at the end of January 1924 by way of New York City. His final entry poignantly records that "new outlooks have presented, new perceptions have developed…. It has been a period of experiences very lonely,

The Green Bench

too, for the most part...."[49] This was Cooper's first major trip since Emma's death, and clearly her companionship was missed. He remained in New York for several weeks, writing to a friend that he was

> pausing on my way to Santa Barbara to settle some matters in this busy and nerve racking city. I long for the tranquility of Santa Barbara.... I wrote to Mr. Harmer to ask if I could get my studio again ... but no answer has yet come. I also wrote about the possibility of getting one of those apartments at the little court on Anacapa.... At this time, I hope to stay quite a while in your midst—I have worked quite hard in Spain and have a lot of studies and sketches which I shall carry into larger canvases....[50]

Cooper did secure a studio at 116 de la Guerra Street and an apartment at 1320 Anacapa Street upon his return.[51] He began to work furiously in preparation for an exhibition that opened at the Fine Arts Gallery, San Diego, in December 1924. Of the fifty-eight works, half were Spanish scenes and half were a fairly eclectic mix of Indian, European, and California pictures. Watercolors made up approximately half of the Spanish pictures.[52] One critic noted that in this medium, "Mr. Cooper has achieved most of the quality of the oil technique with an added subtle delicacy."[53] Among the several major oils was *Segovia, Spain*. This painting shares a lineage with Cooper's earlier cathedral paintings, but his style had now become much freer and his paint handling far more liberal. The viewpoint is probably from atop the Alcazar castle and fortification, which would have allowed a comprehensive panorama of the cathedral. Seen under bright sunlight, the burnt sienna rooftops of the surrounding buildings and the lush landscape in the foreground punctuate the canvas. A critic advised readers weary of life's trials, that an antidote was to be found at the Fine Arts Gallery in Balboa Park, where "heaven in the world [was] depicted by Colin Campbell Cooper's brush." His Spanish pictures were "not a fairy land, not a figment of the imagination, but a land of real trees and stone walls, of buildings used by men and women." Cooper's interpretation was through the "poet's eye."[54]

On the heels of the San Diego exhibition, many of the same paintings were shown at Stendahl Galleries in Los Angeles in March 1925. Antony Anderson, critic for the *Los Angeles Times*, offered encomiums:

> Cooper is not one of those painters who disdains a "subject." He is not afraid of the pictorial. Indeed, he is eager in his constant search for the picturesque, more often when it lurks in hiding in out-of-the-way corners. He is a discoverer of cities. Everybody paints the bulls and the caballeros, the mantillas and the senoritas of Spain. But all these things are incidentals. Bits of bric-a-brac. Not the actual life of the country. At Stendahl

Galleries, where an exhibition of his paintings may now be seen, Cooper shows not only the street scenes for which he is noted, but also a group of Spanish architectural studies and views....[55]

Cooper's exhibition schedule in the mid-to-late 1920s, both in California and elsewhere, remained consistent. He developed relationships in Los Angeles not only with Stendahl, but with Ainslie and Ilsley galleries. Little is known about his marriage in April 1927 to Marie Henriette Frehsee. A brief announcement simply noted that the couple was married in Arizona.[56]

Beginning in the mid-1920s, Cooper began to cultivate another aspect of his career: that of playwright and author. As a young man, he had published short stories and articles, and he continued to write throughout his life. However, during the 1920s, his passion for literature became more focused and serious. He wrote numerous plays, which were reprised by local theater companies in Pasadena, Redlands, and Santa Fe in the late 1920s–30s. Cooper was a founder and president of the local Santa Barbara theater club, The Strollers, which staged several of his plays. And he reviewed theater productions in the local paper, occasionally offering sharp and vitriolic assessments of his peers. By the early 1930s, Cooper had written an autobiography, *In These Old Days*; a historical novel, *Old Ironsides Last Battle Cruise*; and an illustrated book on India, *Pen and Brush in India*.[57]

The year 1929 was particularly eventful, beginning with a one-person exhibition of forty-five paintings at Kievits Galleries in Pasadena. Arthur Millier, Antony Anderson's replacement as the critic for the *Los Angeles Times* (and not especially sympathetic to Impressionism), offered a positive, if tempered, assessment:

This charming show will be much admired. Gentle and refreshing—as though he had the power always to dip into the fountain of youth.... The exhibition bowls no one over, but hangs discreetly on the walls.... There is never shouting or bad taste. Occasionally the paintings do not go much above the level of illustration, but usually there is a discernible loving attention to all parts of the canvas and a close working out of the subtle gradations of color in the reflected light and shadows that bring the pictures ... to pleasant harmony.[58]

After it opened, Cooper and his wife spent nearly eighteen months in Europe visiting many of the haunts of his youth in Italy, France, and England. He rented a studio in Paris for four months beginning in December 1929. According to his diary, the pace of the trip was fairly grueling, but most significant were Cooper's notations of persistent ailments. "I cannot stand at my easel for any length of time without feeling a lack of balance that I should fall if I don't hold on to something," he wrote in October 1929.[59] He complained of shaking, rheumatism,

Late Afternoon, Santa Barbara Mountains

and failing eyesight. "When I stand I hold Marie.... I do not even walk without her even for a short distance...."[60] Nonetheless, he continued to work, preparing sketches, for example, at the cathedrals in Canterbury and Chartres, and at Windsor Castle. They returned to New York in August 1930, remaining only a few days. "New York was hot and stuffy," he wrote. "Four days of it were quite enough. But what a fairy land it is. A few years ago the Woolworth tower stood out as a great landmark. Today with the immensely higher towers it is only one of the smaller ones. Always coming into the harbor the sight has been impressive, but now it is awe inspiring."[61] His delight in architectural wonders had not wavered; the dramatic, changing skyline, punctuated by the increasingly upward trajectory of new and bigger buildings, remained fascinating.

Within a few months of returning to Santa Barbara, Cooper held a small exhibition in his studio. Despite his prolonged absence and the continued erosion of Impressionism's popularity—even in California, where its relevance and importance were sustained far longer than on the East Coast—Cooper's personal appeal had not waned. Supporters applauded his brilliant "technique" and definable "subjects"—criteria that by this date had long been held in contempt by avant-garde artists and critics. Well aware that detractors considered his art retrograde and insipid, Cooper nonetheless held firm in his convictions:

> Art is a great expression of emotion, which covers your attitude toward people and things. It can have no formulas, as it is a registration of reactions. Nevertheless, I don't agree with modern artists. Their theory seems to be that art mustn't look like anything at all, and that there is nothing creative except that evolved from the inner consciousness. That if you paint something material, it is copied art.... They even go so far as to say that technique is nothing. That's misleading to people. They ought to know how to draw, at least. I don't like to see a face with a nose three times too long and a neck out of joint just because the artist's mind happened to conjure it that way.[62]

Cooper's vituperative condemnation of modern art (and contemporary jazz) was underscored in a missive he called "The Open Mind." Whether it was intended for publication is unclear, but it expresses utter disgust for "the cult of ugliness" that characterized the work of abstract painters.[63] Believing "that which is genuine ... will endure always," he hopes that there

Beauvais Cathedral (France)

will be an eventual return to reason and the appreciation of technical excellence and individual expression.

During the 1930s, Cooper exhibited mostly smaller works, as indicated by the prices noted in his account book. The instances of more substantial prices appear to be for works recycled from earlier years. To be sure, this was a terrible time for the art market. In a 1932 letter, art dealer Philip Ilsley reminds Cooper that "it has been our experience that any sales made during the past few months have been made at reductions of at least thirty percent from 1930 prices.... I am sure that you realize that prices of most commodities, even of necessities, have dropped fully fifty percent in the last three years."[64] While Cooper may have intentionally reduced the sizes and prices of his work in response to the market, the changes more likely reflect his declining physical condition. For example, in 1934 the Faulkner Memorial Art Gallery in Santa Barbara hosted an exhibition of seventy-seven works. Over one third of the thirty-three paintings had been done before Cooper settled in California; of the balance, only perhaps five had been completed after 1930. Nevertheless, the show was a smashing success.

Cooper's deteriorating health is reflected in his account book beginning in 1935, when his wife took over the task of recording the entries. Exhibitions in Los Angeles, San Diego, Rochester, and Springville, Utah, contained only recycled pieces. In a poignant twist, Cooper's eyesight failed in the last years of his life, ending his long and heralded career.[65] When he died in November 1937 at the age of eighty-one, his obituary ran in newspapers from New York to Los Angeles, from San Diego to Philadelphia and Rochester, New York.[66] In a moving tribute to his colleague and friend, John Gamble wrote that Cooper "saw beauty wherever he went and joyed in the endeavor to pass on to others through his work some of the pleasure which was his."[67]

Cooper's long and fruitful career was enviable. Subsequent to his death, Faulkner Memorial Art Gallery staged a memorial exhibition in 1938. The images of New York, India, Europe, New England, and California were like the pieces of a large jigsaw puzzle which formed a picture of his life. He was eulogized as a man whose "credo was beauty."[68] Cooper's work was neither simplistic nor unsophisticated. His paintings married a high level of technical acuity with a delight and curiosity in a range of subjects. Through Cooper, the effectiveness of labels—

Mission Santa Barbara

Eastern versus Western American painter—is challenged. His artistic precepts were consistent, regardless of his home address. And his art remains timeless.

Deborah Epstein Solon, Ph.D. is an independent exhibition curator. Her most recent exhibitions, all accompanied by major catalogues, include: East Coast / West Coast and Beyond: Colin Campbell Cooper, American Impressionist (2006) which she co-authored with Dr. Gerdts; Alson Skinner Clark, American Impressionist (2005); and In and Out of California: Travels of American Impressionists (2002). In 2005, Dr. Solon received a silver screen award at the International Film and Video Festival for a documentary she co-wrote and co-produced, Colonies of American Impressionism, based on an exhibition she curated of the same name.

NOTES:

1. Colin Campbell Cooper diary (hereafter CCC diary), 12 March 1914, in Colin Campbell Cooper Family Collection (hereafter CCCFC). The author is indebted to Jennifer Dahlke, the artist's great-grand niece, for generously allowing access to the Cooper Family Papers, which included the artist's diaries, correspondence, and book and play manuscripts, among other personal papers. According to James Hansen, "during his Santa Barbara years, he [Cooper] returned to India and continued as far East as Burma, where he did studies of the Schwedagon Pagoda." Cooper went to Burma during his 1913–14 trip to India; no evidence suggests that he returned to India in the 1920s. See James M. Hansen, *Colin Campbell Cooper*, exhibition catalogue, (Santa Barbara: James M. Hansen, 1981), n. p.

2. Cooper to Macbeth, 21 June 1914, Archives of American Art, Smithsonian Institution, Washington, D. C. (hereafter Archives of American Art), reel NMc35, frame 97. Phil and Marian Kovinick compiled extensive research on Cooper which was graciously loaned courtesy of Ray Redfern, Redfern Gallery (hereafter Kovinick research).

3. See "Poland Spring Exhibition, Twenty-First Summer Show in Maine State Building," Emma Lampert Cooper Papers, Memorial Art Gallery, Rochester, New York, courtesy of Marjorie B. Searl, chief curator, Memorial Art Gallery, Rochester. Ms. Searl has graciously provided extensive research material on both Emma and Colin Campbell Cooper.

4. Cooper to Macbeth, 8 November 1914, Archives of American Art, reel NMcag, frame not available.

5. CCC diary, 1 January, CCCFC.

6. Identifying the Taj Mahal paintings presents a particular problem. According to Gloria Rexford Martin, author of an unpublished exhibition history of the present painting, Cooper executed at least seven renditions of the building, several with similar or identical titles. Extant labels attached to this painting indicate that it was exhibited under at least two titles, *The Taj Mahal*, and *The Taj Mahal, Agra, India*. In a review of the Macbeth exhibition, the writer describes two Taj paintings, one matching the particular cropped viewpoint of the pool seen here. However, the matter is complicated by the fact that another similar version is extant (see Sotheby Parke Bernet, Los Angeles, 18-19 June 1979, lot 170). Martin believes that this painting was probably exhibited at the Macbeth Gallery in New York (1915) and at the Memorial Art Gallery in Rochester, New York (1915) under the title *Taj Mahal Agra (Afternoon)*. Another version of the Taj exhibited at Macbeth, *Taj Mahal Agra (Morning)*, with the more typical axial view, was reproduced in *The Art World*, October 1915. I am grateful to Ms. Martin for graciously sharing her research.

7. For a full description, see Janice Leoshko, "Mausoleum for an Empress," in Pratapaditya Pal et al., *Romance of the Taj Mahal* (New York: Thames and Hudson, 1989), 53-87.

8. It has been suggested that the stone structure to the right of the pool might be a sarcophagus. See Martin research.

9. "Cooper Showing His Pictures of India: Exhibition of Fifteen Canvases the Result of Artist's Recent Eastern Trip—Paintings are Colorful," [1915], unidentified newspaper clipping, CCCFC.

10. Cooper to Macbeth, 8 November 1914, CCCFC.

11. Cooper's account book was graciously provided to the author by Dr. William H. Gerdts.

12. CCC diary, 6 December 1913, CCCFC.

13. "Colin Campbell Cooper's Indian Pictures," unidentified newspaper clipping, CCCFC.

14. For information on the work, see Curatorial Catalogue Sheet, Santa Barbara Museum of Art, California. Among the venues were the Corcoran Gallery of Art, Washington, D.C. (1915), Macbeth Gallery, New York (1915), The Brooklyn Museum, New York (1915), Mystic Art Association, Connecticut (1916), The Art Institute of Chicago (1916), Dallas State Fair (1917), the Pennsylvania Academy of the Fine Arts (1918), and the Faulkner Memorial Art Gallery, Santa Barbara (1934). The painting was reproduced in the *California Graphic*, May 1927.

15. See "India Pictures at Art Gallery: Work of Mr. and Mrs. Colin Campbell Cooper on View," *Rochester Democrat and Chronicle*, 31 October 1915. I thank Marjorie Searl for a transcript of this review.

16. The Palace of Fine Arts remained open until May 1, 1916. See Laura Bride Powers, "Art and Artists About the Bay," *Oakland Tribune*, 2 April 1916, p. 13. Courtesy of Jessie Dunn-Gilbert, The North Point Gallery, San Francisco.

17. Implicit in the fair's conception was the belief that it could elevate the public's taste. According to a critic, "One of the best results to be looked for from the exposition is the effect on public taste in architecture, painting, and sculpture. Here are assembled numerous examples of what is really good art—seen time and again by the people who will enter the gates and grown familiar to the public mind, these cannot fail to mold taste." Ben Macomber, "Exposition Art Bound to Leave Lasting Impression," *San Francisco Chronicle*, 6 June 1915, p. 26. Courtesy of Jesse-Dunn Gilbert, The North Point Gallery, San Francisco.

18. Louis Christian Mullgardt, *The Architecture and Landscape Gardening of the Exposition*, www.books-about-California.com/Pages/PalacesandCourts.

19. Anna Cora Winchell, "Artists and Their Work," *San Francisco Chronicle*, 19 March 1916, p. 19. Courtesy of Jessie Dunn-Gilbert, The North Point Gallery, San Francisco.

20. "Artists Visit City," *Los Angeles Times*, 26 April 1916, section 2, p. 10. The article notes the couple stayed at the Hotel Clark, which may have been a popular spot for artists. Alson and Medora Clark stayed at this hotel when they visited California in 1919. I am grateful to Gloria Rexford Martin for this citation.

21. For a history of Mission San Juan Capistrano, see Pamela-Hallen Gibson, "Mission San Juan Capistrano," in *Romance of the Bells* (Irvine, California: The Irvine Museum, 1995), pp. 45-71.

22. For information on Lummis, see Susan Landauer, "The Culture and Consumption of Plein-Air Painting," *California Impressionists* (Athens, Georgia: Georgia Museum of Art, and Irvine, California: The Irvine Museum, 1996), 36.

23. The attempt to rewrite history, turning the hardships imposed upon the Indians into accounts of benevolent missionaries who transformed aboriginal, uncivilized natives, is highlighted by a series of articles that appeared in *The Californian*. See especially Laura Bridge Powers, "The Missions of California," *The Californian* (September 1892), 547-56. For a lengthy discussion of the mission, see Deborah Epstein Solon, "The Life and Work of Alson Skinner Clark," Ph.D. diss., Graduate School of the City University of New York, 2004.

24. Jean Stern, "Art in California: 1880 to 1930," in *Romance of the Bells*, p. 73.

25. We know that Cooper returned to the mission at least once more, as a small gouache of the church's exterior is dated June 24, 1926 (The Irvine Museum, Irvine, California).

26. Cooper did a similar but smaller gouache from the same perspective of the courtyard. See *Mission San Juan Capistrano*, 1916, gouache on paper, 10 x 12 inches (The Irvine Museum, Irvine, California).

27. The small notice stated that "Colin Campbell Cooper, the New York etcher and painter, has been sketching in the fair grounds at San Diego for several months past. He is so taken with Southern California that in all probability he will open a studio at Laguna Beach and remain there through the summer." See "News and Notes," *Los Angeles Times*, 7 May 1916, p. 3. No evidence supports the claim of a possible Laguna Beach studio.

28. Autobiographical Notes, Artist file, Santa Barbara Museum of Art, CCCFC.

29. Frieseke, Miller, Parker, Guy Rose, Karl Anderson, and Edmund Greacen exhibited together in 1910 at the Madison Art Gallery, where they were dubbed the "Giverny Group," reflecting their residence at the art colony in Giverny, France. See Bruce Weber, *The Giverny Luminists and Their Circle* (New York: Berry-Hill Galleries, 1996).

30. Emma died on July 30, 1920 from tuberculosis. I am grateful to Marjorie Searl for obtaining a copy of her death certificate.

31. See obituary, *The New York Times*, 21 August 1920. It appears she became ill and went to stay with her niece, Esther Steele, a nurse, in Pittsford, New York.

32. Cooper, Autobiographical Notes, CCCFC.

33. For information on Cooper's residences, see Kovinick research.

34. The phrase refers to the title of a book by Carey McWilliams, *Southern California: An Island on the Land* (Los Angeles: Carey McWilliams, 1946; reprint 1973).

35. See my two studies, *Colonies of American Impressionism: Cos Cob, Old Lyme, Shinnecock and Laguna Beach* (Laguna Beach, California: Laguna Art Museum, 1999), and *In and Out of California: Travels of American Impressionists* (Laguna Beach, California: Laguna Art Museum, 2002).

36. See Angela Miller, *The Empire of the Eye: Landscape Representation and American Culture Politics, 1825–1873* (Ithaca, New York: Cornell University Press, 1993), 17, quoted in Charles Eldredge's excellent foreword to Nancy Boas, *The Society of Six* (Berkeley and Los Angeles: University of California Press, 1997), 6.

37. The phrase refers to how the British colonials viewed themselves in relation to the imperial centers. See Eldredge in Ibid.

38. Cooper, unsigned typescript letter, [1933], Santa Barbara Historical Museum, CCCFC.

39. For the development of the Santa Barbara artist colony, see Gloria Rexford Martin and Michael Redmon, "The Santa Barbara School of the Arts," *Noticias* 40 (Autumn and Winter 1994): 45–83.

40. See David F. Myrick, *Montecito and Santa Barbara: The Days of the Great Estates*, vol. 2 (Pasadena, California: Pentrex Media Group, 1991).

41. For a history of the school, see Martin and Redmon.

42. Cooper, Autobiographical Notes, CCCFC.

43. For information on the El Encanto, see Michael Redmon, "History 101: What is the History of the El Encanto Hotel?" *The Independent*, 13 October 1994, p. 76. I am grateful to Michael Redmon, Director of Research and Publications, Santa Barbara Historical Museum, for this citation.

44. Lisa N. Peters, "Cultivated Wildness and Remote Accessibility: American Impressionist View of the Home and Its Grounds," in *Visions of Home* (Carlisle, Pennsylvania: Trout Gallery, 1997); 14.

45. See May Brawley Hill, "The Domestic Garden in American Impressionist Painting," in Ibid., 53–54.

46. In a letter to Macbeth, 20 March 1922, he wrote that "I am just leaving for the Pacific Coast...." Kovinick research. "Colin Campbell Cooper was the guest of Wheel J. Bailey in La Jolla in September and spent many hours sketching in Balboa Park, San Diego," in *California Southland* 33 (October 1922), 3.

47. Before leaving, Cooper gave an enlightening interview reflecting the depth of his concern with his adopted city. "If I am fortunate enough to bring home in my pictures any suggestions that may be helpful to the future city planning of Santa Barbara I shall be only too happy to have performed a service to the city. There is no city in California that is better adapted to the Old Mexican and Spanish traditions of architecture than Santa Barbara. We should preserve those traditions very carefully and build on them, and on them only." "Artist Cooper Going to Spain: Hopes to Bring Back Suggestions of Value to Santa Barbara Plan," unidentified newspaper clipping, CCCFC.

48. CCC diary, 25 June 1923, CCCFC.

49. Ibid., 29 January 1924.

50. Cooper to Litti Paulding, 11 February 1924, CCCFC.

51. "Noted Artist Returns Home," *Santa Barbara Daily News* [1924], CCCFC. Cooper's residence remained 1320 Anacapa Street until 1931 when he moved to number 1715.

52. See *Paintings by Colin Campbell Cooper, N.A.* (San Diego: Fine Arts Gallery, San Diego Museum, 1925).

53. Beatrice de L. Krombach, "Colin Campbell Cooper's Collection (cont.) at Fine Arts Gallery Closes Sunday," unidentified newspaper clipping, CCCFC.

54. H.L.D., "Cooper's Art Takes Jaded Mortal to Glamorous Sphere," 7 December 1924, unidentified newspaper clipping, San Diego Museum of Art artist file, courtesy of D. Scott Atkinson.

55. Antony Anderson, "Of Art and Artists," *Los Angeles Times*, 21 June 1925, p. 12.

56. See *Santa Barbara Morning Press*, 11 March 1927, courtesy of Michael Redmon.

57. According to numerous pieces of correspondence, Cooper made many unsuccessful attempts to have his work published.

58. Arthur Millier, "Of Art and Artists," *Los Angeles Times*, 10 February 1929, section 3, p. 14.

59. CCC diary, 3 October 1929, CCCFC.

60. Ibid., 3 December 1929.

61. Ibid., 3 August 1930.

62. Doris Drake, "Colin Campbell Cooper Tells of His Start and Experiences as an Artist," unidentified newspaper clipping, 14 August 1933, Artist file, Santa Barbara Museum of Art.

63. Colin Campbell Cooper, "The Open Mind," undated typescript, CCCFC.

64. Philip Ilsley to Cooper, 20 October 1932, in ibid.

65. John M. Gamble, "Fellow Artist in Tribute to Cooper," *Santa Barbara News-Press*, 7 November 1937.

66. See, for example, "Colin Cooper, Artist, Died," *Santa Barbara News-Press*, November 7, 1937, p. 1; "C. C. Cooper, Artist, Dead in West at 81," *The New York Times*, 7 November 1937, section II, p. 9; "Art Colony Dean Dies," *Los Angeles Times*, 7 November 1937.

67. Gamble.

68. "Colin Campbell Cooper, Artist, Died," *Santa Barbara News-Press*.

chronology

1856	Born in Philadelphia, Pennsylvania to Dr. Colin Campbell Cooper and Emily Williams Cooper
1878-79	Joined the Philadelphia Sketch Club; began exhibiting with the Philadelphia Society of Artists
1879	Enrolled in the Pennsylvania Academy of the Fine Arts; studied under Thomas Eakins
1881	Traveled to Colorado & New Mexico; painted near Colorado Springs and in Taos
1886	Sketching trip to Holland & Belgium
1889-90	In Europe; studied in Paris at the Académies Julian, Delacluse and Viti; traveled to Spain & Algiers
1895-98	Instructor in watercolor, Drexel Institute, Philadelphia
1896	Much of his work destroyed in a fire at Hazeltine Galleries, Philadelphia
1897	Married fellow artist Emma E. Lampert
1902	Began series of skyscraper paintings
1904	Juror, Louisiana Purchase Exposition, St. Louis
1908	Elected Associate, National Academy of Design
1912	Coopers on board the RMS *Carpathia* during the rescue of *Titanic* survivors; painted the rescue operation
1912	Elected Member, National Academy of Design
1913	First trip to India
1915-16	Wintered in California; attended Panama-Pacific International Exhibition, San Francisco; visited Yosemite, Los Angeles and Panama-California International Exposition, San Diego
1920	Wife Emma died
1921	Moved to Santa Barbara; became dean of painting at the Santa Barbara School of the Arts
1922	Juror for National Academy of Design Annual Exhibition
1927	Married Marie Henriette Frehsee
1929-30	Coopers in Italy, France and England
1937	Died in Santa Barbara, CA

awards (selected list)

1895	Bronze Medal, Atlanta Exposition
1903	W.T. Evans Prize, American Water Color Society
1904	Gold Medal, Pennsylvania Academy of the Fine Arts
1904	Seinan Prize, Philadelphia Academy of the Fine Arts
1905	Gold Medal, Art Club of Philadelphia
1910	Bronze Medal, Dallas State Fair, TX
1910	Silver Medal, International Fine Arts Exposition, Buenos Aires
1911	Beal Prize, New York Water Color Club
1915	Gold Medal (oil), and Silver Medal (watercolor) Panama-Pacific International Exposition, San Francisco
1918-19	Walter Lippincott Prize, Pennsylvania Academy of Fine Arts

collections (selected list)

Art Institute of Chicago
Boston Museum of Fine Arts
Brooklyn Museum
City of Santa Barbara
Crocker Art Museum, Sacramento, CA
Dallas Museum of Art
Irvine Museum, Irvine, CA
Musee de la Cooperation Franco-Americaine, Bierancourt, France
Memorial Art Gallery, University of Rochester, NY
Metropolitan Museum of Art, New York
New York Historical Society
Oakland Museum of California
Pennsylvania Academy of the Fine Arts, Philadelphia
Reading Public Museum, PA
Saint Louis Art Museum, MO
San Diego Museum of Art, CA
Santa Barbara Museum of Art
The White House, Washington, D.C.

affiliations

American Watercolor Society, New York
Art Club of Philadelphia
California Art Club
National Academy of Design, New York
New York Society of Painters
New York Water Color Club
Philadelphia Water Color Club
Salamagundi Club, New York
Santa Barbara Art Club

paintings in the exhibition

Taj Mahal, Afternoon, c1913
Oil
29 x 36 in.
Courtesy private collection, Santa Barbara

Palace Gate, Udaipur, India, 1914
Oil
36.3 x 46.2 in.
Courtesy Santa Barbara Museum of Art, gift of the artist's family

Malines Cathedral (Belgium)
Oil
45 x 33 in.
Courtesy Santa Barbara Women's Club

Beauvais Cathedral (France), 1926
Oil
45 x 33 in.
Courtesy Sullivan Goss - An American Gallery, Santa Barbara

Segovia, Spain, 1924
Oil
36 x 33 in.
Courtesy Santa Barbara Museum of Art, gift of the artist's family

Venetian Scene, c1902–1912
Oil
18.2 x 25.8 in.
Courtesy Santa Barbara Museum of Art, gift of the artist's family

View of the City and Lincoln Cathedral (England), c1905
Oil
17 x 21.5 in.
Courtesy Robert & Christine Emmons, Santa Barbara

The Train Round House, Salem, Massachusetts, 1895
Gouache
20 x 25.5 in.
Courtesy David G. Kaplan, Foster Park, CA

Terrace at Martha's Vineyard
Oil
18 x 15 in.
Courtesy Mr. & Mrs. Thomas B. Stiles, II, Monarch, CA

House in Martha's Vineyard
Gouache
15 x 18 in.
Courtesy Mr. & Mrs. Thomas B. Stiles, II, Monarch, CA

Pennsylvania Avenue (Washington, D.C.)

Gloria Rexford Martin

Juxtaposing the majestic architecture of the nation's center of government with the quotidian life of the streets would also inspire Colin Campbell Cooper, for the recently discovered *Pennsylvania Avenue (Washington, D.C.)* celebrates the ceremonial core of America, historic Pennsylvania Avenue, NW, that connects the White House to the awe-inspiring Capitol, here resplendent in the distance at the dawn of the twentieth century. In the foreground, Cooper captures from a high vantage point the crossroads of the Avenue with 10th and D streets, a site he may have selected in part to honor his birthplace of Philadelphia. A statue of fellow Pennsylvanian Benjamin Franklin, commissioned by *The Washington Post* founder and editor, Stilson Hutchins, from Jacques Jouvenal (1829-1905), stands at the heart of the plaza in the intersection. Behind this 1889 sculpture rises the Trader's National Bank Building. Originally designed in 1871 by Philadelphia architect John Fraser and first called Vernon Row, the complex would house many artists' studios as well as the Art School of the Washington Art Club during the last quarter of the nineteenth century. In charge would be Edmund Clarence Messer, future Director of the Corcoran School of Art.

A June 14, 1903 review in *The Washington Post* of a private showing revealed that the "distinguished Philadelphia artist" had just spent three weeks in the city, where he painted "three very remarkable watercolors of the Capitol Building." The reviewer gave the title of only one work, "*Capitol by Moonlight*," and described the second piece as "a near-by-view of the building" in which "the Senate wing occupies the foreground." The third watercolor—"a pure 'plein air' study of the Avenue with the Capitol in the distance, taken from one of the windows of the *Evening Star's* composing room" at 1101 Pennsylvania Avenue—probably served as a preliminary study for this oil on canvas, also created in 1903. That same year the Art Club of Philadelphia included the oil in their *Fifteenth Annual Exhibition of Oil Paintings and Sculpture* and illustrated it in the accompanying catalogue. An advisory committee then selected the striking, sunlit *Pennsylvania Avenue (Washington, D. C.)* for exhibition in the Fine Arts Palace of the Louisiana Purchase International Exposition at St Louis in 1904.*

Gloria Rexford Martin has served as a consulting curator at the Santa Barbara Museum of Art and is currently writing a monograph on the American muralist and modernist Richard Haines. She has curated and written the principal essays for several exhibitions, including Focus on the Figure: Southern California Artists (1850-1950); and A Painter's Paradise: Artists and the California Landscape (1996). She has published numerous articles and has lectured extensively on California Tonalism and Modernism. She received her M. A. in Art History from Stanford University.

*Vernon Row, redesigned at least twice, was demolished in the 1960s and replaced by the J. Edgar Hoover Building (headquarters of the Federal Bureau of Investigation); the sculpture was moved to Pennsylvania Avenue and 12th Street, NW. The writer wishes to thank Lida Churchville, Research Librarian, Historical Society of Washington, D.C., and Barbara Bahny, Public Relations Director, Willard InterContinental Hotel for their valuable assistance.

Pennsylvania Avenue, Washington, D.C., 1903
Oil
21 x 25.5 in.
Courtesy Mr. & Mrs. Frederick C. Groos, Jr., San Antonio, TX

Fifth Avenue, New York City, 1906
Oil
39 x 27 in.
Courtesy New-York Historical Society, Museum purchase, James B. Wilbur Fund

The Financial District, Manhatten, c1908
Oil
32 x 19.5 in.
Courtesy Mr. & Mrs. Thomas B. Stiles, II, Monarch, CA

Flat Iron Building, 1904
Casein
48.8 x 28.9 in.
Courtesy Dallas Museum of Art, Dallas Art Association purchase

Mountains of Manhattan, c1903
Oil
42 x 68.5 in.
Courtesy City of Santa Barbara, gift of the artist

Hudson River Waterfront, 1902–1921
Oil
36 x 29 in.
Courtesy New-York Historical Society, gift of Miss Helene F. Seeley,
in memory of the artist & his wife

San Francisco Panama-Pacific Exposition, c1916
Oil
19 x 22 in.
Private collection, courtesy The Irvine Museum, Irvine, CA

An Afternoon Stroll, Balboa Park, 1916
Gouache
17 x 20.8 in.
Courtesy Redfern Gallery, Laguna Beach, CA

Mission San Juan Capistrano, c1916
Gouache
36 x 46 in.
Courtesy City of Santa Barbara, gift of the artist

Mission Courtyard (San Juan Capistrano), c1916
Oil
17.5 x 22.5 in.
Private collection, courtesy The Irvine Museum, Irvine, CA

The Rustic Gate, c1918
Oil
46 x 36 in.
Courtesy The Irvine Museum, Irvine, CA

Mission Santa Barbara, 1921
Gouache
6 x 8.5 in.
Courtesy private collection, Santa Barbara

Late Afternoon, Santa Barbara Mountains
Oil
15.5 x 18.5 in.
Courtesy private collection, Sherman Oaks, CA

A Santa Barbara Courtyard, c1925
Oil
15.5 x 18 in.
Santa Barbara Historical Museum, gift of Helene F. Seeley,

Untitled - Blue Mandarin Coat
Gouache
14 x 11 in.
Courtesy Mr. & Mrs. Thomas B. Stiles, II, Monarch, CA

The Lotus Pool, El Encanto, Santa Barbara, c1921
Oil
36 x 29 in.
Courtesy Reading Public Museum, Reading, PA

The Green Bench (Harmer Adobe), c1922
Oil
15 x 18 in.
Courtesy Louise Clarke & John Carbon, Santa Barbara

Tea Party (preliminary study for *Tea Time*)
Oil
12 x 15 in.
Courtesy Quackenbush & Winkler, Santa Barbara

Tea Time, Samarkand Hotel, 1921
Oil
36 x 46 in.
Courtesy Lawrence Beebe, Palm Desert, CA

Terrace at Samarkand Hotel
Oil
14 x 20 in.
Courtesy Mr. & Mrs. Thomas B. Stiles, II, Monarch, CA

The Terrace at Samarkand, 1927
Oil
36 x 46 in.
Courtesy John & Patty Dilks, Carmel, CA

Samarkand Hotel, c1925
Oil
16 x 20 in.
Courtesy Dr. & Mrs. Kelly Tucker, Villa Park, CA

Basket of Dahlias, c1922
Oil
36 x 29 in.
Courtesy De Ru's Fine Arts, Laguna Beach, CA

Half Dome, Yosemite, 1916
Oil
25 x 30 in.
Courtesy Paul & Kathleen Bagley, Princeton, NJ

64

A Santa Barbara House
Oil, 9 x 12 in.
Courtesy George Stern Fine Arts, West Hollywood, CA

Santa Barbara Sunset
Gouache, 5 x 7 in.
Courtesy Gloria Rexford Martin, Santa Barbara